Kids' Random Acts of Kindness

Kids'
Random Acts
of
Kindness

Foreword by
Rosalynn Carter

Introduction by
Dawna Markova, Ph.D.

CONARI PRESS
Berkeley, California

Conari Press books are distributed by Publishers Group West

Printed in the United States of America
Cover: Sharon Smith Design; illustration: Ann Jackson; lettering: Lily Lee
Interior illustrations: Joan Edwards

ISBN: 0-943233-62-3

Library of Congress Cataloging-in-Publication Data

Kid's random acts of kindness / the editors of Conari Press ; foreword by Rosalynn Carter; introduction by Dawna Markova.
     p. cm.
  ISBN 0-943233-62-3 (pbk.) : $8.95
  1. Kindness—Case studies—Juvenile literature. 2. Altruism in children—Case studies—Juvenile literature. 3. Helping behavior in children—Case studies—Juvenile literature. 4. Children—Conduct of life. I. Conari Press.
BJ1533.K5K53 1994
177'.7'083—dc20   93-46050
                                                                CIP
                                                                AC

Contents

A little girl was late getting home from school and her mother began to scold her, but then stopped and asked, "Why are you so late?"

"I had to help another girl. She was in trouble," explained the daughter.

"What did you do?"

"Oh, I sat down and helped her cry."

Acknowledgements

Our deepest thanks and appreciation to all the children, parents, teachers and schools listed below for sharing their stories, enthusiasm and committment to bring more kindness into the world. The list that follows is only a small selection from the thousands of letters we received. Also, our "interpretation" of the spelling of some names might be as wildly inaccurate as some of the handwriting was creative.

Christ Church Day School · Haidian Teacher Training School · J.W. Parker Middle School · Greentree Elementary School · Southampton Middle School · Lockhart Elementary School · Duniway Middle School · McDonogh School · Martin Meylin Middle School · Bel Aire School · Seville Elementary School · Franklin School · Denison Middle School · Alki Middle School · Finn Hill Jr. High School · McIntyre School · Coleytown Elementary School · Burckhalter School · Brookville High School · Wisconsin Dells High School · Christina

Landsman · Christy Abousy · Renee Freismuth · Stacie B. Green ·
George Aure · Chaminique Ragland · Josh Bates · Mike McCabe · Holley
Shahidy · Dawn Raenee · Phiet Tran · David Eskalein · David Soariner ·
Mario Boyd · Jacob Marsh · Joel Fumia · Shelly Glennon · Carol Bichel ·
Michel Yau · Omar Perodona · Aaron Greeley · Jeremy Costello ·
Nicholas Fumia · Jessica Forman · Rachel Salerio · Justin Courtright ·
Nadirah Bradshaw · Steve B. · Steven Hambleton · Michael DeBakey ·
Danny Della Maggiore · Jacqui Tingvall · Geno Fumia · Andew Adix ·
Krista Kipp · Michael McKay · Ian Jacobs · Meghan McMackin ·
Elizabeth Gerrish · Carl Bennett · Tiona Bennett · Tiffany Hines ·
Ganice Allen · Richard Jones · Tawanda Henley · Randi Jones ·
Takiyah Bullock · Latrina Reuben · Terri Benson · Gregory Smith ·
Zane Lundy III · Lakieda Bennett · Raeshawnda Boyd · James Jackson ·
Shamika Darby · Leila Smith · Robert Lomax · Latia Davison · Laren
Thorton · Bryan Anderson · Erica Dennis · Robert Moore · Dolores
Wiggins · La'aja Wiggins · Jessica Morris · Justin Booker · Isaac
Harrison · Catherine Caines · Marcus Jones · Christina Preston ·
Sherese Reese · Eric Hearn · Jackie Robinson · Bobby Coleman ·
Steven Coleman · Shatora Robinson · Terrance Jamison · Ladonna
Dixon · Mary Djin · Daniel Fancher · Alonda Fontanez · Donell
Gooden · Derron Green · Ernest Hall · Takisha Jenkins · Robert Jones ·
Kevin Morgan · Lakesha Purter · Mrs. Wilkes · Ms. Wartella ·
Dr. Davis · Allen Green · Kenny Townsend · Jarret Morgan · Travis
Shavers · Richard Johns · Tommie Lynn Wall · Lakesha Maxshure ·

Marcus Procter · Fatimah Hall · Lance Dugger · Melanie Johnson · Dwight Tucker · Maria Hall · Vince Eggleton · Lamont Flemister · Monica "Cuppy" Jones · Cornell Whitley · Dean Smalley · George Smalley · Myron Baldwin · Richard Hutsherson · Travis L. Fenton · Dewayne Mahaffey · Robert Smith · Ronald Gavins · Willie Blair · Davon Allison · Jermaine Davis · Rick Rock · Tony Baldwin · Tommy Blackwell · Eugene Bailey · Louis Gilliam · Terry Cook · Stacy Martin · Leonard Williams · Mike Hepler · Aaron Mickens · Ian Candy · Denis Candy · Kimberlee Sowers · Andrew Jacobs · Courtney Vaughn · Shu Pei Ng · Our Friend Jack · J.J. · Michael Lyons · Josh Osborne · Anne Sklar · Courtney Fehn · Lisa Erskine · Lauren Kimball · Cathy Busha · Jeffrey Ng · Jeffrey Chen · Colleen Horn · Dominic Rivera · Kyle Gray · Christian Fumia · Natasha G. · Matthew Bachmann · Mary Urban · Rania Kfuri · Janet Metzger · Paul Kirk · Andy Bartholomew · Jean Bartholomew · Ben Minden

Foreword

One of the most rewarding tasks in life is to teach our children, and in teaching them, to learn again some simple truths about ourselves. In the words of the children in this book, kindness is the connection that links us all together and strengthens the bonds within our communities, neighborhoods, and families.

We have all observed how easily and genuinely kindness flows from children—the sharing of favorite foods or dandelions picked off the lawn, the offering of toys, the sincerely-felt concern over wounds suffered by others. Simple acts of kindness are natural to children.

With their innocence and total dependence on others they instinctively know that we are all part of a large community.

It is this quality that makes a child's smile melt our hearts. But it is also a quality that is fragile and easily crushed if not respected, nurtured, and appreciated. So much in our culture teaches us fear, to retreat behind high and wide walls for protection, and restrict our connection to the larger community.

The world can seem like such a frightening place that we often suppress the innocent beauty of our children's sense of kindness by our own anxieties, justified in the name of protection. The tragic result is fewer connections, less sense of community, and ultimately less hope. To strip away the spontaneous exuberance and kindness of children is a disservice to them and even more a disservice to humanity.

Kids' Random Acts of Kindness allows us to take a small but very important first step, that of extending one hand to another and in turn, making kindness a regular part of our lives. This book allows us to celebrate the joy of connecting with another person, while encouraging the impulse in our children.

It is written in Isaiah that "a little child shall lead them." May we all follow the example of these children.

Rosalynn Carter

Introduction

(Warning—Do not give this book to children, do not read it or show it to them, unless you are willing to connect with your own heart and foster a basic attitude of generosity and compassion in them.)

I heard a true story the other day about a boy and his sister, told to me by a doctor. The girl, aged eight, had a rare disease, and only her six-year-old brother had the kind of blood she needed to live. His mother asked him if he would be willing to donate blood to save his sister's life. He said he'd have to think about it.

After a while, he returned and agreed to the transfusion. Both children went to the clinic together. The doctor had them lay down on adjoining beds, and drew blood from the boy until the plastic transfusion bag was full, then transferred the bag over to the sister, allowing it to drip slowly into her arm. As his sister was receiving his blood, the brother called the doctor over and whispered in his ear, "Will I start to die right away?" The boy thought that giving blood to his sister meant that he would be giving up his life for her—that was why he needed to think about it.

Thirty years of working with children, teaching them and learning from them in the darkest corners of the inner city and the shiniest arenas of the suburbs has led me to believe that the compassionate generosity of that boy is present at the core of every one of us. I'm not talking about the ledger sheet one-for-you-one-for-me giving we have learned as adults, but the kind of giving to you that is also a giving to me, the letting go that opens body and spirit. I think what we most long for is who we are at our core, and children are the truest mirrors of that open-hearted nature.

Lean in and look at what they reflect back to us:

Kids are hopeful, they believe they can change, easily and often. They look forward, not back. They like to think about what could be, not what was. If you ask them the reasons they did something last night, they'll tell you how they'll do it differently tomorrow.

Kids are possibility addicts. Tomorrow they'll hit a home run, the day after they'll get along with their sister, next year they'll get a nicer teacher. They're always working on something. If you listen deeply, you'll hear a language of hopefulness and striving, an elasticity that keeps them going and trying.

Kids organically love to master challenges. They want to try new things, move in new directions, be productive. They are genuine risk takers, sometimes out of faith, sometimes out of desperation. More than anything else, children want and need to belong, to partner, to collaborate.

Kids teach us how, with a positive focus and strong support, we can move forward in a healthy direction. But what are we offering to them? When most of us were children, the adults around us believed that the future would be better than the past. Nowadays, kids are being educated in a context in which the adults around them believe the future will be worse than the present. We are crushing our children with our own pessimism and cynicism.

Research has shown that children who are raised by parents whose aim is to teach them to avoid negative situations—"Be careful, you'll get hurt"; "Try harder or you'll fail"—tend to be defensive, isolated, and overall low achievers, seeing the world as a dangerous place to be avoided. On the other hand, children whose parents demonstrate and support active engagement in the community, who teach and reinforce a positive model of interaction with the world, become high achievers.

In other words, if we only focus on what's wrong, we will produce another generation of inhibited, hoarding, hardening, refusing adults who do their very best to avoid problems but have no vision of what they need to move forward. But it doesn't have to be that way. It's not just problems that we face, but what these problems can become that matter.

As adults, we must ask more of our children than they know how to ask of themselves. What can we do that will foster their open-hearted hopefulness, engage their need to collaborate, be an incentive to utilize their natural competency and compassion? What if instead of condemning the darkness, we turn our children toward the light by giving them something to move towards? What if we show them ways they can connect, reach out, weave themselves into the web of relationships that is called community? What if we helped children expand their repertoire by offering them new possibilities for forward movement so they could learn to translate their anger, rebellion, defiance into an active challenge they could be proud of? What is destructiveness but creativity looking for a place to happen? What is stubbornness but determination seeking soil in which to root?

Generosity is an inherent motivator of the greatest power, which will emerge if given a chance. To experience it is rewarding and self-reinforcing, not just for what it produces, but for the inner feeling we get that we can make a difference. Once begun, generosity starts a landslide because success strengthens children.

To help children feel good about themselves, we have to help them feel good about the world. We must learn again to hope and encourage them to do the same. For as soon as you say, "I hope this will happen," what follows is "This is what I can do about it." Merely telling them over and over that they are wonderful won't do a thing to increase their self-esteem—did it ever work for you?—but give them a map and an engaging project that is relevant, and it will serve as a lightening rod for their energy. Watch the power that is released!

When the adult version of *Random Acts Of Kindness* was first published, hundreds of teachers across the country were captivated by the vision it offered. They gave assignments to their students to write about such unsolicited acts that they had experienced or created. Schools in Maryland, Florida, California, Washington, and Texas initiated school-wide programs promoting "Random Acts of Kindness." The results were so rich that teachers sent them to Conari Press, who was then induced to seek out more. They advertised in *Merlin's Pen*, a teacher's magazine, and put out a call for stories on a teacher's computer bulletin board. Like a sunrise, the light would not be held back: stories poured in; from big cities to rural communities, from private academies to ghetto schools throughout Canada and the United States, children of all ages responded enthusiastically.

The drive-by shootings, the senseless destruction and violence has not stopped. This book is an attempt to balance that, not deny it. We need to teach children how to connect what is best in them with what the community around them needs. The bridge that is built will lead them to a place of belonging where the healthy part of them can be activated, where forward momentum can be fostered, where they can learn again to dream of a better world that is theirs to create. It is in the spirit of that possibility that this book is born.

—Dawna Markova, Ph.D.,
author of *How Your Child is Smart, The Art of the Possible,* and *No Enemies Within.*

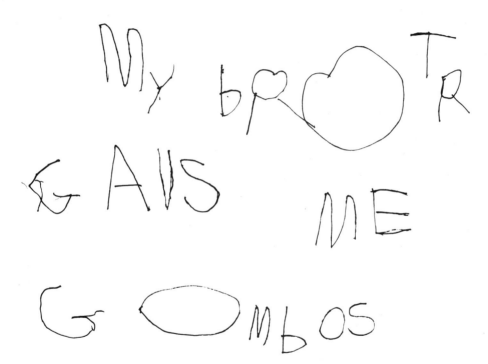

(My brother gave me gumballs.)
—Valerie, 1st Grade

It was a bright sunny day.
My Dad and I got up in the
morning. We got dressed and went
for breakfast. When we got there
the waitress tormented me. but
I didn't torment her. That was
my random Act of kindness

—Steven, 6th Grade

At school I gave a girl some chips and the next day she gave me some chips and candy just for giving her some chips. Now am I nice or what.

—Alexandria, 6th Grade

When I was sick with the the chicken pox the time Jessie gave them to me. I went to my mom's best friend her name is Judie but I call her Unt Judie. She gave me a Troll im a hospatel unaform that read: GET WELL SOUN! and I liked the chicken pox!

—Lindsay, 2nd Grade

Last year I had a lot of headaches but they never went away. I went to doctors but they didn't help. I didn't know what to do. I began to get sad about this as my headaches became more painful and more often. It was hard to do a lot of things if you don't feel good. The person who really helped me was my mom. She took care of me and told me everything would be alright. My mom is my random act of kindness.

—Jessica, 5th Grade

I give cookies and other
food to friends
during lunch if they
are having a
bad day.

—Carl, 4th Grade

A week ago my mother took my brother, my cousins, and I to the movies and my mom didn't have enough money to pay for my cousins and I luckely I had twenty dollar bill in my pocket and I paid for my cousin and I. I cost me $9.45 but it was nothing

COUSINS (2) $6.30
me   + $3.15
        ─────────
         $9.45

—Aaron, 5th Grade

One day my family and I were going to a baseball game and it was pretty cold out. In the city there's alot of homeless people. We saw this one guy with some dogs and you could see there ribs.

There were no bottles around him so we assumed he didn't spend all the money he gots on beer and stuff. He was selling bracelets for 25 cents. We bought a few and gave him $50.00. I wish nobody lived on the streets.

—Josh, 5th Grade

My class joined an "anonomous Santa" program and adopted a mother and her four children. At firsty we each brought in a few cans of food (the usual donation). But as Christmas grew nearer, our class began to realize just how needed and important our gits would be. Then the presents really started coming in. When I woke up Chritsmas omrning I though of our family opening their presents and how surprised they would be and that was my best christmas present.

—Lily, 8th Grade

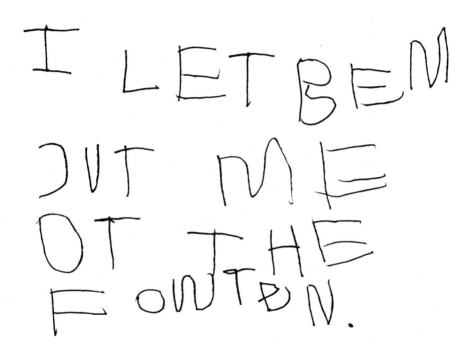

I LET BEM
JUT ME
OT THE
F ONTDN.

(I let Ben cut me to the Fountain.)
—Thanas, 1st Grade

I got the money from a bank I have $976.56 in my bank. I'm going to buy my mom 2 presents on her birthday. Don't tell her

—Steven, 4th Grade

I went to a Norweigon bakery that had no business. I ordered a French Dip and out of their kindness they gave me a big peace of the best chocolate cake then they showed me around. They told me they were a couple that moved to Norway because it was too cold. when I left

I was stimulated.

—Alexander, 5th Grade

Friday night my sister was going to the game she needed some sneakers. She asked me could she wear my Reeboks. and most of the time we can't get along with her, but I let her wear my Reeboks.

—Nadirah, 6th Grade

Last year I was involved in a toy drive for children. My mom got me to do it and I was not very excited. The only reason I was doing it was for extra credit in school. I spent day after day sorting toys and looking for the clock to say it was time to go home. I went to basketball practice the night of the wrapping and I got to the school just a little bit late.   I was stunned to see over a hundred and fifty people there wrapping gifts. I started to feel good about what I had done.

All the help and good will that was shown that night really touched my heart. I hope that i will have the chance to do that again. The biggest surprise is that i didn't care about the extra credit any more, to this day I haven't turned in the sheet.

—Kyle, 8th Grade

I did a Kind Random act of Kindness. I woked up and herd my sister saying milk, milk. In stead waking my mom up I went down stares and wormed my sisters milk and gave it to her. The End.

—Maik, 5th Grade

Two of my friends entered a science fair and both were sure to win. But the night before the judging, one of my friends projects fell to pieces. The other friend stayed up all night helping to fix it and they actually made it better.

Because my friend helped make it better he lost the competition, but felt good because he had helped someone in need.

—David, 8th Grade

I once gave my friend a suprise party. I did it because the day it was her birthday her parents were too busy moving to another house. She was pretty sad so I decided to give her a suprise birthday party. She was so happy that she cried.

—Lisa, 7th Grade

I went to the toy shop. I was looking for a special toy so was a boy. Mom saw one and got it down from the top shelf. And then I went the boy and gave it to the boy.

—Justin, 4th Grade

Once I gave my big sister something for her birthday. And she did not except it. She told me that she did not want any thing that I gave her. After she told me that I felt realy bad because I

→

always do nice
things for her and she
always treats me bad.
Except on my birthday she
rote me a letter it said:
(Sometimes I may treat you
bad but Deep down in the
Ocean I Love you aton)

—Sheraina, 3rd Grade

In early October I found out that my golden retriever had cancer and that she would have to be put to sleep. I was really sad. We went with her to the vet. she was really happy to be with her family, she had no idea what was going on. I felt really bad. We were all crying hard. I had her for eleven years. The vet was very sympathetic. we decided to have her body cremated.

When we went back to

the vet to pick up her ashes they showed us a box. When we got home we opened the box. Instead of her ashes, that we expected to see, there was a silver tin. There was a small white envelope placed at the bottom of the box. Inside, there was a ten dollars and a note from the vet. He said that he was very sorry and to use the money to get some ice cream or a treat for the family.

—Meghan, 7th Grade

In forth grade I saw a guy named Loni, he was being made fun of because he is a little on the ~~large side~~ size. People were asking him if he wanted a chili burger and stuff like that. I helped him out and from that day till about halfway nthrough sisth grade I've been called a fat ~~boyfriend~~ and a meatloaf lover. Loni is cool and we are friends to this day.

—David, 7th Grade

Last year my Dad died and some kids in my class would put notes and candy and stuff in my box. It made me feel good but sometimes I cried.
I don't know why.

—Brian, 4th Grade

Each year I pretend I believe in Santa Claus so my cousin enjoys Christmas more. She likes Santa and still believes. I personally dont believe in Santa Claus, but she does.
I hope, someday she figures it out, but for now its our secret.

—Jacob, 6th Grade

One day my sister was cleaning out her closet when she found a card that was signed by our brother who had died seven years ago. We were very upset and didn't want to talk to anyone.

Then a guy that my sister was friends with called to talk to my sister. My sister didn't want to talk and when he found out why he didn't insist on talking.

Later that night a car pulled up in front of our house, we thought it was our parents coming home but it was Andy, my sister's friend. He came in with three chocolate milkshakes for us. He talked to us for a while and told us jokes and made us laugh. We stayed up till 11:00 and then he left. →

He probably doesn't know this but even though we were so stuborn and didn't want to talk, we felt a lot better after we talked to someone. But he didn't make us forget about our brother, he made us love more.

—Krista, 7th Grade

My friend lives next to a shopping mall.
Every time her mother drove by the
mall she saw the same homeless man
on the bench. He didn't even have a
blanket. She went out and bought
him a nice blanket and a pillow and gave
it to him. Ever since he waves at her
and smiles when he sees her.

—Stacie, 8th Grade

I did a Random act of kindness. I wrote to Rachel that I hope she has a nice <u>day</u> and I think she is a nice <u>day</u> (I also taped a <u>jolly</u> rancher and an eraser to the note).

—Renee, 5th Grade

Random acts of kindness no matter how small make a difference. For instance, in school if I hold the door for someone who has a popped binder or say to so someone, especially if that person is teased, that they look nice or I like their hair or something they wore, it could make their day. That to me would be better than having a day full of terrible things.

—Marne, 7th Grade

One random act of kindness that my dad did was since we had moved to California we were so far away from are relitives and we were so homesick my dad told my mom and I that he had a surprise for us! We had no idea what it was. My Dad told my Mom and I to come into the living room. there was nothing their! Then all of the sudden my great grand ma walked in!

—Sarah, 5th Grade

I like reading newspapers. Every day we go to a gas station to go to get a newspaper to read. When I went out of the gas station, I noticed a woman coming. Now usually being myself, I **never** hold doors for anyone. But feeling good that particular day, I felt like doing something nice. Now you may think this is nothing, but I think that someday the little things will count in this world.

—Michael, 6th Grade

My random act of kindness is small but pretty good. Everyday say at least one kind thing to everyone you talk to. This isn't hard to do and it make you and the people that you talk to feel good.

—Brad, 5th Grade

Often I used to go to downtown.
I'd see people wearing old rags and
alot of time no shoes. By now
you could figure out that these
people are home less. I also see
commercials on the subject. I
don't go downtown anymore but if I
did I'd give the first one I saw
all the money I had.

—David, 6th Grade

Mi Busr m mea Lef Pile InG then hlet me.

(My brother made me a leaf pile and he let me jump in it.)
—Brad, 1st Grade

Maybe if everybody in the world did something nice every day, instead of planning out the begininig Of a war or worrying about how much power they have under their belts, I think the world would be a much nicer place for us fut ure leaders and the ones behind us. It would also lessen the amount of wrong that my generation has to fix. To the adults that could care less about

what happens in the future because
they won't be there or to the ones
that continue to make the world an
even more terrible place to live by
destroying it. STOP AND THINK, not just
about what you are doing, but what
it will do in the long run of time.
About what you are doing or it will be
like for your future descendents.
WE CAN'T FIX EVERYTHING.

—Christy, 8th Grade

The one important Act of Kindness that I have done is I went to an old folks home. When I went there I played some checkers and some board game to cheer them up. I let them win.

—Danny, 7th Grade

Once I caught my finger in the door.
My mom rushed me to the hospital.
the doctor put 11 stiches in my
finger. I was scared of my stiches.
the doctor told me some jokes, and then
I didn't feel anything because
I was paying attention to the jokes

—Andrew, 2nd Grade

The nicest thing I ever did was in December of 1992 it was my birthday I was nice to my family even to the people I did not like. I want to go back to Mexico again to be nice to the People I don't like because I love Mexico.

—Ronnie, 6th Grade

kindness is not always shown with money. One day I got a lot of stuffed animals and I tucke them to a or funige and that is my storie.

—Jeremy, 5th Grade

Every month or so we change seats in our science/math block. One of these particular change days I was really down. Not only because we had to change seats but because most of my friends decided to get mad at me at the same time.

I ended up sitting across the room from all

friends. the girl behind me asked why I looked so sad. I told her and as we talked I realized what a nice person she was.

I started to become aware how much she touched peoples lives, including mine, all the time. Every time she was close enough to talk to someone she →

made it a point to help,
make them feel better or
love, or just talk to that
person.

Since I have met her
I have tried to be a
nicer person. It isn't always
easy, in fact sometimes it is
hard, but every time I get
discouraged I look at the
big smile on her face.

—Elizabeth, 7th Grade

Once I went to a baseball game and Bip Roberts hit a fly ball. The man next me caught the ball. Then gave it to me. that made me feel great.

—Tommy, 4th Grade

Once or twice a year my family and I go to Gladmomorial in San Francise. It's a place (church) where everyday volenteers go help and feed the homeless. And a couple special times of the year like Christmas and thanksgiving They have a big blow out. anyway back to where I started, my family and I volenter to help serve food

→

and pass out eating utensels.
One year a very special little girl
no older than 10 years old gave me
flowers. Till this day I still have
the flowers. I'll always remember
that girl.

—Sylvia, 7th Grade

To me a random act of kindness means in your own special way doing something that makes the world a better place. I think if everyone would commit themselves to doing a kind act the world would run a little smoother.

—George, 6th Grade

A peer in my school wore a very beautiful necklace every day. Of course, glitter on plastic was beautiful to a kindegardener. But her necklace was different. It had brilliant corolors of Indain-made beads and gold and silver balls in between.

One day she was playing tag and a rowdy boy yankend off her necklace. Beads went flying everywhere as the little girl burst into tears.

→

I didn't know her very well, so I stayed on the monkey bars. I could see that the boy felt awful as he tried to help her find the scattered beads. It was hopeless.

The next day, she had no necklace so I took off my glitter on plastic necklace and gave it to her. I knew it wasn't as pretty, but my heart ached to see such a bear neck.

She wore my glitter and plastic necklace with pride for the rest of the year.

—Jacqui, 7th Grade

One day I came upon an elderly neighbor that desparately needed help weeding her garden. After many hours of labor she offered me ten dollars. I said "What the heck, this ones on me." It felt good helping her out of the goodness of my heart.

—Michelle, 6th Grade

I was learning how to field a
ground ball like a real infielder.
My brother was like an infielder
from heaven to me then. Not coming
up on a short-hop, watching the
ball into his glove and keeping
his tailgate down. His soft hands
scooping up the ball like an
ice cream scooper, scooping
smoothly through the ice cream.
When it was my turn to try, it
was like I was just born.

→

After about half an hour of ground balls I was getting the hang of it. The next sunday at Majors tryouts I did what he told me to do. I got a call that night saying I was on the Pirates. I'd made it to the Majors! If it weren't for my big brother, I don't know where I'd be right now!

—Michael, 7th Grade

Once at the grosherey stor this lady cluden't park her car because there was a cart in the way so I moved it so she could park her car and she thankd me for doning that

—Rachel, 5th Grade

When you frens are picing on wone of your other frens, you sticke up for you other frend and tell them to stop saying that.

—Omar, 5th Grade

When I was in 3rd Grade the whole school were playing B-I-N-G-O. I was new in that school. After 15 minutes I yelled B-I-N-G-O and they took me to the office to get a prize but when I got there they said I couldn't get a prize just because I was new in that school. I felt bad, my heart was broken into little pieces they took me back to class. A girl who had won a prize went up to me and gave me her prize I felt good.

—Patricia, 6th Grade

I do a Random Act of Kindness almost everyday. I laugh out loud to my friends and my funny teacher Miss Miles and share my smile generously.

—Michael, 4th Grade

Once when I was in pre-school there was this girl that didn't speak english and I taught her how to speak english.

—Jessica, 5th Grade

One day I went to
Kisen hospital for my yearly
shots. When I saw a guy that
was Italian in a bed looking
like he is about to die. He
had cancer I noticed know
one was visiting him. So
I went to give him some
company. He seemed to
have a smile on his face
when I was taking to
him.

—Steve, 7th Grade

Once I was holding Sniffer and I let him run around. The next thing I know Sniffer is gone. Glenn comes in and helps find. He made me feel happy.

P.S. Sniff is a hamster.

—Evan, 4th Grade

I was going down the stairs after 1st period. Everyone was walking all over a fifth grader on the ground. I decided to help him pick up his books and when I was finished I told him I'm sorry everyone was stepping on him. I walked away feeling good about myself but I knew he was crying. I know how he felt. I was

→

also a fifth grader once. I'm not telling you this so you think I'm a nice person. I'm telling you this because what i did made me feel good about myself. I hope you take that into consideration. I want other peopel to know that by helping one person it makes you feel like you helped the whole world.

—Irin, 8th Grade

At night my mom always comes into my room, says goodnight, gives me a kiss, and goes into her room to read or watch t.v.. On particular night, she came in and did her usual and left. About an hour later, I heard my door open. It was my mom. She walked over to my bed, gave me a big hug and kiss and told me she loved me. Then she walked out. The next morning I asked her why she did that and she said, "I just wanted you to know I loved you."

—Kimberlee, 7th Grade

flat out nice

My school had a Random Acts of Kindness program and I thought it would just go about their usual business. I was wrong. People became more aware of others and more willing to help, holding doors, helping to pick up books, limiting the number of cutdowns and just being flat out nice. It gives me hope that the world's wounds can be healed if we all committ random acts of kindness.

—Lisa, 8th Grade

When my cousin came to live with me
I had to share my room with him.
My dad would say be nice to him
because his parents are far away
in Veitnam, so I introduced him to
my friends, they liked him a lot.
He started to get on my nerves
but I was able to keep my anger
to myself, When he moved we started
to become best friends. My random act
of kindness was that I wasn't his
worst enemy any more I was his
best friend. So there is a lot of
ways to show kindness. Ones that have
to be done by movement an ones that
come from the heart.

—Phiet, 6th Grade

Today Reese picked

a burr of my back.

—Dane, 2nd Grade

Our school asked for candy for the Christmas pinata. I thought how nice it would be to get chocolate instead of candy that barely anybody likes. So I put in Milky Ways, Three Musketears, Reeses Peanut butter cups and Snickers. It was a small deed but it stuck in my head.

—Sara, 6th Grade

On mother's day you a to give you mother some thing nice and If you don't do that at lease tell her happy Mother's day and if you don't do neither of those I don't know what to tell you.

—Maurice, 5th Grade

Where do We Go From Here?

The publication of *Random Acts of Kindness* triggered an extraordinary groundswell across the country. It seems that in the midst of what often appears to be a growing swirl of indifference throughout society, we are all quietly longing for a world in which kindness can and does play a more vital role.

Of the tens of thousands of fascinating responses we received, none was more powerfully moving than the outpouring of efforts from children. We were delighted by their straight-forward, shoot-from-the-hip, no-nonsense approach. We were moved by the depth of feeling, the passion and urgency that emerged so clearly from their stories—almost as if they sensed somehow that we are entering a time in which a return to kindness and a connection to community is no longer a luxury but a necessity if we are to survive the span of their lifetimes. In short, the letters we received sounded suspiciously like the opening salvos in a Children's Crusade of the 1990's— stirring, beautiful, committed, and powerful.

Here are excerpts from the letters of eighth graders at McDonogh School in Baltimore, Maryland: "We've been practicing 'Random Acts of Kindness' for a couple weeks and I have noticed major changes in the eighth grade itself"; "At first I was surprised that such a small action could make a difference in my attitude and my classmates. As a week or two went by, most people were helping everyone"; "I couldn't think of anything I did nice. Then it hit me. It wasn't once act. It was a whole lot of acts. Things like giving people a pencil if they needed one, lending books and other little kind things. It improved the mood of the school." "The acts that were the nicest and most effective were the so-called small acts. Things like holding the door or helping someone pick up books they've dropped. I felt these were the most effective because they became habits—even after the movement has settled down, we still do these simple acts of kindness. And I think that was the whole idea."

One of the most moving responses was the creation of "Random Acts of Kindness" (RAOK) gangs among inner-city children in Pittsburgh. Organized with the help of Denis Candy under the auspices of the Boys and Girls Clubs of Western Pennsylvania, these RAOK gangs sprung up like wildflowers emerging from the cracks in the sidewalk. The kids chose names like "The Gladiators," "BHC," "Bedford," "The Mysteries," "The Hill," "The Mailman's" "R.C.'s," and "B.C.'s," and drew up their own rules like "Respect Due to All; Trust, Honesty—that's the way it's gonna be; No Clowning; No Put Downs;

No Profanity; No Touching if You Don't Want to Be Touched." They wrote RAOK gang rap songs and devised elaborate schemes for spreading kindness throughout their neighborhood—setting an example that struck a powerful chord with us.

Rap Song of the B.H.C.
by Lakesh Maxshure and Tommie Lynn Walls

Conflict Resolution is where it's at
So listen as I begin to rap
'Cos you are you and I am me
But we are us and us are we.

Identify the problem, bring it out
Don't kick or punch or even shout
Attack the problem not the fear

Listen with an open mind and ear.
'Cos you are you and I am me
But we are us and us are we.

Focus on the problem, don't leave it behind
Treat others with respect, feeling kind
Take responsibility for your actions
and you'll get a feeling of a satisfaction.
'Cos you are you and I am me
But we are us and us are me.

Not listening to others is really unhip
So listen to me and I'll give you a tip
No bossing, no threatening, no putting down names
No making excuses, no passing the blame.
'Cos you are you and I am me
But we are us and us are we.

Bringing up the past is not very cool
So whoever does it is really a fool
And getting even is really unkind
Don't use your hands, only your minds,
'Cos you are you and I am me
But we are us and us are we.

If push comes to shove just fill it with love
If push comes to shove just fill it with love
'Cos you are you and I am me
But we are us and us are we.

Obviously this is only a beginning—we don't pretend that such actions alone will end violence in this society. But it is a beginning. We encourage you to think creatively about how you can use the "Random Acts of Kindness" concept to make a difference in your community. Can you join with youth organizations to help form alternatives to violent gangs? What about senior centers and nursing homes?—our elders need purposes for living too.

Write us and let us know what you come up with so we can pass your ideas on to others. Also, we would be happy to provide copies of either *Random Acts of Kindness* or *Kids' Random Act of Kindness* at quantity discounts for use by local groups in spreading the word. Call us at 800-685-9595.

Additionally, because we feel so strongly about the need for kindness in our communities, we are offering a free teacher's guide to Random Acts, and a free packet of information about how you, your church, or community group can create a Random Acts of Kindness day. See the following pages for full details.

With the publication of this book and our other materials on Random Acts of Kindness, we hope in some small way to provide encouragement for parents, teachers, and especially children to have the courage and commitment to bring into being a crusade of kindness that will ripple outward and swell into a tidal wave that cannot be ignored.

Free Teacher's Guide to Random Acts of Kindness

We're offering an easy-to-use, inspirational guide for educators on how to teach a unit on random acts of kindness in the classroom. It includes the latest research on the physiological and psychological effects of doing good, a list of suggested activities, and information on how to get involved with other participating schools across the country. Send for your free copy!

Teacher's Guide
Conari Press
1144 65th St. Suite B
Emeryville, CA 94608

Random Acts of Kindness Day

Write us for your free packet on how to host a Random Acts of Kindness Day for your neighborhood, school, city, state, or household, and learn how to join up with the ongoing national kindness movement:

Random Acts of Kindness Day
Conari Press
1144 65th St. Suite B
Emeryville, CA 94608